T0113870

THE
LEGACY
FACTOR

AMY G. PHILIPP

WESTBOW
PRESS®
A DIVISION OF THOMAS NELSON
& ZONDERVAN

WestBow Press books may be ordered through booksellers or by contacting:

WestBow Press
A Division of Thomas Nelson & Zondervan
1663 Liberty Drive
Bloomington, IN 47403
www.westbowpress.com
844-714-3454

ISBN: 978-1-6642-7853-0 (sc)
ISBN: 978-1-6642-7854-7 (e)

Library of Congress Control Number: 2022917326

Print information available on the last page.

WestBow Press rev. date: 09/28/2022

Contents

Foreword

As water reflects the face, so one's life reflects the heart.
(Proverbs 27:19 NIV)

Dedication

This book was written with the hope that all who read it will know the Good News as well as benefit from the wisdom and guidance provided by the Wonderful Counselor and the Prince of Peace.

Acknowledgements

First and foremost, I give thanks to God for His holy Word, my access to it, and the grace by which I have been saved. I extend heartfelt appreciation and thanks to Kenisha Bethea for her keen eye and editing expertise as well as her willingness to take on my project during a busy season of life.

I am also sincerely grateful for the cover art provided by my daughter, A.B. Moore, the manuscript feedback provided by Ruth Snyder, and for Greg Keith's time, insight, and encouragement.

Introduction

When I was in the seventh grade, one of my homework assignments was to write an obituary for Julius Caesar. Most of my classmates and I didn't know what in the world an obituary was, so our teacher told us to find a newspaper and look up the obituary section so we could read a few examples.

Easy enough. Those were the days when many families in my community received a morning and an evening newspaper. I quickly found several obituaries, and I referenced their format to write and submit one for the Roman Emperor. A few days later, I was disappointed to learn that I received a low grade on the assignment because I didn't include the cause of Caesar's death. I chatted with my teacher about it and shared that none of the obituaries I read listed a cause of death, so I thought it was probably inappropriate to include it. Fortunately, she took that into consideration and gave me the opportunity to revise what I wrote.

To this day, many obituaries do not mention a cause of death. Often, a reader can make assumptions about how a person died from various information included in such a post. And, much is often revealed about a person's life, priorities, accomplishments, and contributions.

Over the years, I've read many more obituaries of friends, relatives, strangers, and even celebrities. They are basically a condensed form of my two favorite genres of literature—biographies and spiritual memoirs. They appeal to me because I'm relational; I like to meet people, and I'm curious about their drivers. Such posts as well as online tributes and condolences provide readers with a succinct glimpse of a person's life, how they were perceived by others—even themselves—and what kind of information was chosen for inclusion.

I've determined that although such summaries and commentaries about a life may be short, **one's legacy and its impact last much longer.** Varying viewpoints, outlooks, and beliefs affect the shape of an individual's personal legacy, as well as how much one may consciously care about how he or she wants to be remembered. And while carefully crafted words serve to provide a brief record that memorializes a life, they cannot wholly convey the tangible impact that someone's life had on others.

The amount of time and where it was invested, significant *or insignificant* interactions with others, and shared experiences are the weighty factors that contribute to the kind of legacy one may leave. I heard the following quote by Maya Angelou a few years ago, and I find it to be quite true: "I've learned that people will forget what you said, people will forget what you did, but people will never forget how you made them feel."

Emotions are such a powerful part of the human experience. Consider how *Google's* English dictionary provided by Oxford Languages defines the word emotion: "instinctive or intuitive feeling as distinguished from reasoning or knowledge." How we feel is a heart-based, synthesized emotional response to what we hear or experience. We can read to gain cognitive knowledge, but direct experience and interaction with someone involves many of our senses and thus has a more profound effect in regard to what we glean from it.

Can you think of an experience in your life or a connection with another person that elicits strong emotions? What thoughts come to mind when you recall the experience or the relationship? What was it about your interaction with that person that impacted you?

I think all of us can recall an experience or two that were either positive or negative. Since most of us would like to forget the negative ones and enjoy more positive ones, some thought should go into how we interact with people and what kind of company we may want to keep. That being said, is there someone in your life whom you would describe as being "good" company? What is it about that person that makes him or her fall into that category?

Would you fall into that category? I hope that I would, and because it matters to me, I've put some thought into what priorities and pursuits in life will contribute to the personal legacy I want to leave.

Priorities and Pursuits

As a follower of Jesus Christ, my faith journey has served to reveal foundational priorities and pursuits that are often counter-cultural. However, these personal "drivers" enable and equip me to navigate all that encompasses my daily life with more peace, perspective, and wisdom—qualities that are also mutually beneficial to others. Because of that, I think they are worth sharing.

So, what are the faith-related drivers that I've found to be helpful in building a meaningful legacy? They fall into the following three categories that we'll interactively explore using *logos, God's Word as revealed in the Bible,* as a guide:

1. The **pursuit of knowledge** that reveals God's character, will, and ways
2. The **practical application** of acquired knowledge about God's will and ways
3. The **acknowledgement and correction** of attitudes, behavior, or perspective that are antithetical to God's will and ways

The Pursuit of Knowledge that Reveals God's Character, Will, and Ways

Logos to Explore:

Consequently, **faith** comes from hearing the **message**, and the message is heard through **the word about Christ.** (Romans 10:17 NIV; emphasis mine)

The farmer sows the **word**. Some people are like seed along the path, where the **word** is sown. As soon as they hear it, Satan comes and takes away the **word** that was sown in them. Others, like seed sown on rocky places, hear the **word** and at once receive it with joy. But since they have no root, they last only a short time. When trouble or persecution comes because of the **word**, they quickly fall away. Still others, like seed sown among thorns, hear the **word**; but the worries of this life, the deceitfulness of wealth and the desires for other things come in and choke the

word, making it unfruitful. Others, like seed sown on good soil, hear the **word**, accept it, and produce a crop—some thirty, some sixty, some a hundred times what was sown." (Mark 4:14–20 NIV; emphasis mine)

Reflect and Respond

Think about the words **message** and **word** in the verses above. What is the connection? How are they related?

Describe how you think faith is developed through hearing the message.

What is the word about Christ? (See Romans 3:23–24, John 3:16–17, and Romans 3:27.)

Where can you go to learn more information about the **message** and increase your faith-based knowledge?

In sum, the word about Christ is the gospel. Hearing and accepting the gospel changes hearts and brings a greater understanding of God's Word. This is because the Holy Spirit accompanies the free gift of salvation offered through belief in Jesus Christ as Savior. The indwelling presence of the Holy Spirit in believers provides greater understanding, clarity, wisdom, and perspective.

Related Logos to Explore:

Peter replied, "Repent and be baptized, every one of you, in the name of Jesus Christ for the forgiveness of your sins. **And you will receive the gift of the Holy Spirit.**" (Acts 2:38 NIV; emphasis mine)

But the Helper, the Holy Spirit, whom the Father will send in My name, **He will teach you all things that I said to you.** (John 14:26 NASB; emphasis mine)

Those who are spiritual can evaluate all things, but they themselves cannot be evaluated by others. For, "Who can know the LORD's thoughts? Who knows enough to teach him?" **But we understand these things, for we have the mind of Christ.** (1 Corinthians 2:15–16 NLT; emphasis mine)

And I will ask the Father, and He will give you another advocate to help you **and be with you forever—The Spirit of truth.** The world cannot see him, because it neither sees him nor knows him. But you know him, for he lives with you and will be in you. (John 14:16–17 NIV; emphasis mine)

(See also Ephesians 1:13–14, 1 Corinthians 2:12–14, and John 16:13.)

I can't think of any other free gift that keeps on giving and has the capacity to equip us throughout our lives. Not only do believers have a unique capacity to understand

God's Word, but they also have a mind for processing and responding to things that happen in their daily lives.

I can recall when I didn't fully comprehend Biblical content. When I was first exposed to the parables, representational teaching stories in the Bible, I took them at face value. Honestly, because of where I was in my spiritual journey, I didn't really find any deeper meaning in them apart from the cultural analogies they illustrated. It's interesting to note that

Old Testament prophecy was fulfilled when Jesus spoke in parables (Psalm 78:2–4), and that it was understood that they could be hard to understand.

Related Logos:

He replied, "You are permitted to understand the secret of the kingdom of God. But I use parables for everything I say to outsiders, so that the Scriptures might be fulfilled: (Mark 4:11–12a NLT)

Then he added, "Pay close attention to what you hear. The closer you listen, the more understanding you will be given—and you will receive even more. **To those who listen to my teaching, more understanding will be given.** But for those who are not listening, even what little understanding they have will be taken away from them. (Mark 4:24–25 NLT; emphasis mine)

Reflect and Respond

We've learned that faith is developed from hearing the word about Christ and how listening to Christ's teaching adds to our understanding. How would you explain or describe the secret to understanding the kingdom of God?

Dig Deeper

Reread the parable shared previously (Mark 4:14–20). It provides us with a good example of how the choice to seek and listen to God's Word grows faith in constructive and impactful ways.

As I considered the agricultural analogy regarding the farmer, sowing seeds, and how they are developed in good soil, I could immediately relate to it because my husband likes to grow produce. Prior to planting his garden each spring, he turns and amends the soil because he wants the seeds that he plants to take root and grow. He travels quite a bit for work, and when he is away and it hasn't rained, he asks me to water what he planted. He understands what contributes to the cultivation and healthy harvest of his garden. Likewise, my faith and its impact on my life will not grow and develop in a healthy and meaningful way if I don't "water" my faith by seeking and internalizing the wisdom and instruction found in **God's Word, which I call the organic fertilizer of faith.**

The good news is that accessing God's Word is easier than ever today. Subscriptions to many biblically-based devotions are free and come straight to email inboxes. Finding out what Scripture shares about various topics is just a click away on our phones, and following pastors and Bible teachers on social media feeds can provide great nuggets that keep us immersed in the nutrients of God's Word throughout the day.

And, if we need an incentive to actively seek and read God's Word, it's encouraging to know that God promises to respond and reward those who actively look for Him.

Related Logos:

Ask and it will be given to you; seek and you will find; knock and the door will be opened to you. For everyone who asks receives; the one who seeks finds; and to the one who knocks, the door will be opened. (Matthew 7:7–8 NIV)

And without faith it is impossible to please God, because anyone who comes to him must believe that he exists and that **he rewards those who earnestly seek him.** (Hebrews 11:6 NIV; emphasis mine)

There are so many content-related distractions that we face every day. News feeds, social media, email, texts, gripping Netflix dramas, etc., all vie for our attention. Though it's been an evolution, I've developed the habit of starting my day by reading three Scriptural devotionals. They come to my inbox each morning, and I read them on my phone with my morning coffee before I look at anything else.

Logos:

Your words were found, and I ate them, and your words became to me a joy and the delight of my heart, for I am called by your name, O LORD, God of hosts. (Jeremiah 15:16 ESV)

His Words are indeed the best way to prime one's heart for the day. And, although I've put systems in place that include reading God's Word as part of my waking routine, I haven't been as devotedly consistent about *starting* the day thoughtfully communicating with God in prayer. The combination of both pursuits is essential, as the mixture provides perspective that extends beyond individual, limited, and often biased or myopic outlooks. Just as eyeglasses improve vision, **reading God's Word and praying** are the spiritual lenses that increase clarity and build discernment as we view and process what's happening in the world. The following Scripture sheds light on the complementary, dual pursuits.

Related Logos about God's Word:

All Scripture is inspired by God and is useful to teach us what is true and to make us realize what is wrong in our lives. It corrects us when we are wrong and teaches us to do what is right. (2 Timothy 3:16 NLT)

For the word of God is alive and active. Sharper than any double-edged sword, it penetrates even to dividing soul and spirit, joints and marrow; **it judges the thoughts and**

attitudes of the heart. (Hebrews 4:12 NIV; emphasis mine)

A person may think their own ways are right. **But the LORD weighs the heart.** (Proverbs 21:2 NIV; emphasis mine)

Reflect and Respond

How do you think the Lord weighs the heart?

How would you explain how God's Word is alive and active, and how does it impact your life?

Related Logos about Prayer:

The LORD is near to all who call on him, **to all who call on him in truth**. (Psalm 145:18 NIV; emphasis mine)

Reflect and Respond

The verse above is short and simple, but so powerful. How can forward progress be made if we're not willing to deal with what may be encumbering us? And the thing is, He already knows it all. What do you think it means to call on Him in truth?

Logos:

Nothing in all creation is hidden from God. Everything is naked and exposed before his eyes, and he is the one to whom we are accountable." (Hebrews 4:13 NLT)

When you ask, you do not receive, because you ask with the **wrong motives**, that you may spend what you get on your pleasures. (James 4:3 NIV)

Therefore **confess your sins to each other** and pray for each other so that you may be healed. **The prayer of a righteous person is powerful and effective.** (James 5:16 NIV)

Reflect and Respond

Considering the verses above, what is an essential aspect of coming before the Lord in prayer? Why?

Logos:

I urge, then, first of all, that petitions, prayers, intercession and thanksgiving be made for all people**—for kings and all those in authority, that we may live peaceful and quiet lives in all godliness and holiness. (1 Timothy 2:1–2 NIV; emphasis mine)

Devote yourselves to prayer, **being watchful and thankful**. (Colossians 4:2 NIV; emphasis mine)

When we have concern for ALL people and consider them each day in our conversations with the Lord, our perspectives and mindsets will shift. When we choose to take things to God in prayer with an expectant, trusting, contrite, and grateful heart, we can have peace and confidence in knowing that God will handle it.

Logos:

This is the confidence we have in approaching God: that if we ask anything according to his will, he hears us. (1 John 5:14 NIV)

Trust in the LORD with all your heart; do not depend on your own understanding. Seek his will in all you do, and he will show you which path to take. (Proverbs 3:5–6 NLT)

Do not be anxious about anything, but in every situation, by prayer and petition, with thanksgiving, present your requests to God. And the peace of God, which transcends all understanding, will guard your hearts and your minds in Christ Jesus. (Philippians 4:6–7 NIV)

And, there's more encouraging truth. When we're just not sure how to pray for someone or something, we have an advocate, The Helper, Whom we can call on for assistance.

Related Logos to Explore:

In the same way, the Spirit helps us in our weakness. **We do not know what we ought to pray for, but the Spirit himself intercedes for us** through wordless groans. (Romans 8:26 NIV; emphasis mine)

In sum, because God's Word is alive and active, when we ingest its nutritious content daily, we will learn from it, and we will be sustained by it. Fueling our tanks with God's Word and giving Him our hearts and minds through reverent and attentive prayer allows God to cultivate us in ways that glorify Him as well as benefit others.

Reflect and Respond

Can you think of an example of a time that you may have had an issue, concern, viewpoint, or perspective that changed or evolved when you shared it with God in prayer and sought to view it from a biblical perspective, or as Jesus Christ would? I certainly have, and I recognize that my **evolution** as a pursuer of what Christ embodies, **also known as a sanctification process**, is what made the difference.

Sanctification is a heady, theological word. What does it mean? The following verses shed light on the concept.

Logos:

Do not conform to the pattern of this world, but **be transformed by the renewing of your mind.** Then you will be able to test and approve what God's will is—his good, pleasing and perfect will. (Romans 12:2 NIV)

Instead, we will speak the truth in love, **growing in every way more and more like Christ**, who is the head of his body, the church. (Ephesians 4:15 NLT)

Since you have heard about Jesus and have learned the truth that comes from him, throw off your old sinful nature and your former way of life, which is corrupted by lust and deception. Instead, **let the Spirit renew your thoughts and attitudes**. (Ephesians 4:21-23 NLT)

Sanctify them by the truth; your word is truth. (John 17:17 NIV)

Reflect and Respond

Which words in the verses above help you to better understand the sanctification process?

How would you describe it?

Who is instrumental in guiding the sanctification process?

How do you access or hear the Holy Spirit? (See Acts 2:38, Ephesians 1:13–14, and John 14:26)

How does truth sanctify believers?

We have to know what God's Word says as well as embrace and *apply* it in order for it to meaningfully impact our lives. None of us is perfect, and we struggle with different things. God is aware of our innate sin natures, and He has a grace-based plan to manage it. We can only benefit from His management plan if we actively participate in it.

The Application Process

Early in my career, I was an elementary school art teacher. As I readied my classroom at the start of a school year, I came across a free poster in a resource room that contained key takeaways from Robert Fulghum's New York Times bestselling book, *All I Really Need to Know I Learned in Kindergarten*. I hung the poster on a wall behind my desk, and to this day, I still find his message about the importance of sharing, playing fairly, saying sorry, etc., to be meaningful.

At the time, I appreciated the simplicity of Fulghum's tenets, as I found them to be universal, foundational principles. As I consider them now, what I find interesting is that such basics do indeed need to be taught, modeled, and practiced as many are in direct opposition to human nature.

Similarly, once we learn God's precepts and values from His textbook, the Bible, we need to practice them and put them to use in our daily interactions with others. I liken it to how I learned to prepare and teach a lesson:

First, I presented a concept and provided various facts or information about it. Next, I provided an opportunity for students to tangibly experience the content I shared through an activity or project.

As the students participated in the activity and sought to solve problems and/or apply what they learned, their active involvement in the activity allowed them to internalize and absorb the information in personal and meaningful ways.

Without initial information or instructions to process, the successful completion of the task would be questionable. And, without the input, support, and feedback from an instructor, many students would experience frustration during the activity phase.

Our spiritual development is much the same. We need to be exposed to God's content, practice it, and evaluate how it was applied in our daily lives. Sometimes, we need to make corrections. That's all part of the learning process.

And, one thing is for sure. None of us is perfect, and none of us live our lives earning good grades on everything that we do. The good news is God knows that. What He desires is a contrite heart. He can work with that. And, the more He has of our hearts, the more we will have a desire to please Him and not grieve His Holy Spirit.

Related Logos:

As it is written: "There is no one righteous, not even one; (Romans 3:10 NIV)

I want to do what is good, but I don't. I don't want to do what is wrong, but I do it anyway. (Romans 7:19 NLT)

The sacrifice you desire is a broken spirit. You will not reject a broken and repentant heart, O God. (Psalm 51:17 NLT)

And I will give you a new heart, and I will put a new spirit in you. I will take out your stony, stubborn heart and give you a tender, responsive heart. (Ezekiel 36:26 NLT)

For you were continually straying like sheep, but now you have returned to the Shepherd and Guardian of your souls. (1 Peter 2:25 NASB)

Reflect and Respond

What is a sacrifice?

How is a broken spirit sacrificial?

How does it make you feel that God doesn't reject us when we admit that we messed up?

Who is the Shepherd and Overseer of your soul?

Although I can't say that I loved every aspect of being a teacher, the parts of the job that were hard for me obviously served a purpose because I have yet another educational comparison to share:

Classroom management proved to be challenging for me. Learning how to effectively motivate and lead a classroom full of different personalities and learning styles was not something that I learned from education classes in college. That's definitely something I would call experiential, on-the-job training—sort of like parenthood. (Fun, fun!) I learned that students will push the envelope, break rules, and try your patience. I eventually learned that positive reinforcement and redirecting behaviors in a relational, grace-based way was more effective than punitive, consequential measures. That's obviously something that God already knew. What a blessing it is to know that we can come to Him when we mess up, make mistakes, and do things that we shouldn't do.

Related Logos:

If we confess our sins, he is faithful and just and will forgive us our sins and purify us from all unrighteousness. (1 John 1:9 NIV)

Therefore, there is now no condemnation for those who are in Christ Jesus. (Romans 8:1 NIV)

Coming to God and owning our mistakes is essential for our spiritual growth as is aligning ourselves with Him and letting Him guide and lead us.

Related Logos:

Then Jesus said, "Come to me, all of you who are weary and carry heavy burdens, and I will give you rest. Take my yoke upon you. Let me teach you, because I am humble and gentle at heart, and you will find rest for your souls. For my yoke is easy to bear, and the burden **I give you is light**. (Matthew 11:28–30 NLT; emphasis mine)

Reflect and Respond

Describe or explain the yoke and burden mentioned above.

Yokes were used on oxen for steering and guidance. Aligning ourselves with God as our guiding yoke should be a welcome and comfortable attachment. Because we have forgiveness in Jesus Christ, our burdens and shortcomings need not weigh heavily upon us once we share them with Him. Because of Jesus Christ's sacrificial death on the cross for us, our sin was His burden. *(It's important to note that different types of sin have different worldly consequences that may impact our relationships with others. Owning our wrongs and apologizing for them helps to heal, restore, and redeem relationships, and feeling the conviction of the Holy Spirit is instrumental in transforming our future behavior.)*

The Bible is rich with many of God's gentle, yoke-guiding, teaching principles that benefit us and others when practically applied. Let's explore some.

God's Yoke in Action

Logos:

Oh, the **joys** of those who do not follow the advice of the wicked, or stand around with sinners, or join in with mockers. But they delight in the law of the LORD, meditating on it day and night. (Psalm 1:1–2 NLT; emphasis mine)

Let love and faithfulness never leave you; bind them around your neck, write them on the tablet of your heart. Then you will **win favor and a good name in the sight of God and man**. (Proverbs 3:3–4 NIV; emphasis mine)

Keep this Book of the Law always on your lips; meditate on it day and night, so that you may be careful to do everything written in it. **Then you will be prosperous and successful.** (Joshua 1:8 NIV; emphasis mine)

Reflect and Respond

What comes from keeping our focus on God's Word, and will, and ways?

Logos:

Jesus replied: "'Love the Lord your God with all your heart and with all your soul and with all your mind.' This is the first and greatest commandment. And the second is like it: 'Love your neighbor as yourself.' All the Law and the Prophets hang on these two commandments." (Matthew 22:37–40 NIV)

Reflect and Respond

When you consider the ten commandments, sometimes it's hard to recite all of them. The verses above basically tell us that all of the law stems from the first two commandments.

What do you think that means, and why do you think those verses are foundational in regard to our conduct and interaction with others?

How are they foundational in setting the tone for other commandments that address stealing, coveting, adultery, etc.?

Logos:

Above all, love each other deeply, because love covers over a multitude of sins. (1 Peter 4:8 NIV)

My command is this: Love each other as I have loved you. (John 15:12 NIV)

Be kind and compassionate to one another, forgiving each other, just as in Christ God forgave you. (Ephesians 4:32 NIV)

Reflect and Respond

It can be hard to love others all the time. What gives us motivational perspective to interact with others in a loving way?

Logos:

No, O people, the LORD has told you what is good, and this is what he requires of you: to do what is right, to love mercy, and to walk humbly with your God. (Micah 6:8 NLT)

Reflect and Respond

When we notice injustice, how should we respond? Would you say that is an immediate, natural response?

What can we do to ensure that we respond to situations in ways that honor God?

Logos:

But I tell you, love your enemies and pray for those who persecute you. (Matthew 5:44 NIV)

Reflect and Respond

Uh, wow, right? Loving your enemies seems to go against human nature, but how does praying for your enemies benefit all involved?

Logos:

Do not take revenge, my dear friends, but leave room for God's wrath, for it is written: "It is mine to avenge; I will repay," says the Lord. (Romans 12:19 NIV)

Reflect and Respond

God's timing and plans may not be the same as ours, but when we trust Him and let Him intercede and manage issues that arise, He assures us that He will take care of it. In what ways is letting God take care of a desire for revenge more beneficial to all involved than how we would handle it?

Logos:

Do not let any unwholesome talk come out of your mouths, **but only what is helpful for building others up** according to their needs, that it may benefit those who listen. (Ephesians 4:29 NIV; emphasis mine)

And do not grieve the Holy Spirit, with whom you were sealed for the day of redemption. (Ephesians 4:30 NIV; emphasis mine)

Get rid of all bitterness, rage and anger, brawling and slander, along with every form of malice. (Ephesians 4:31 NIV)

When words are many, transgression is not lacking, but whoever **restrains** his lips is prudent. (Proverbs 10:19 ESV; emphasis mine)

My dear brothers and sisters, take note of this: Everyone should be **quick to listen, slow to speak**, **and slow to become angry**, because human anger does not produce the righteousness that God desires. (James 1:19 20 NIV; emphasis mine)

Reflect and Respond

There are many more verses about controlling what we say and the danger and fallout from not keeping our mouths shut. As human beings, talking is an integral part of our lives. What wisdom is imparted in the verses above that is helpful to managing our tongues and using our words wisely?

Logos:

We demolish arguments and every pretension that sets itself up against the knowledge of God, and we **take**

captive every thought to make it obedient to Christ.
(2 Corinthians 10:5 NIV; emphasis mine)

Instead, let the Spirit renew your thoughts and attitudes.
(Ephesians 4:23 NLT)

Reflect and Respond

How do the instructions in the verses above resonate
with you?

How difficult do you think it is for most human beings to
consistently follow them?

What do you think is helpful to successfully living them out?

How does capturing the thoughts that enter our minds
about various people and situations and giving them to God
in prayer help to adjust our perspectives?

Logos:

Stand your ground, putting on the **belt of truth** and the
body armor of God's righteousness. For shoes, put on
the **peace that comes from the Good News** so that you
will be fully prepared. In addition to all of these, hold up
the **shield of faith** to stop the fiery arrows of the devil. **Put
on salvation as your helmet**, and **take the sword of the
Spirit, which is the word of God.** (Ephesians 6:14–17
NLT; emphasis mine)

Reflect and Respond

The verses above describe how believers should equip themselves for living life. Describe each of the pieces of armored protection. How is each important? How do they work in conjunction with one another to contribute to success in life and how we interact with others and strengthen our faith?

Logos:

I am the true vine, and my Father is the gardener. He cuts off every branch in me that bears no fruit, while every branch that does bear fruit he prunes so that it will be even more fruitful. (John 15:1–2 NIV)

I am the vine; you are the branches. If you remain in me and I in you, you will bear much fruit; apart from me you can do nothing. (John 15:5 NIV)

Reflect and Respond

Who is the vine? (For more context, read all of John 15.)

How would you describe someone who is fruitful?

What are the attributes of a person who displays the fruit of the Spirit? (See Galatians 5:22–23.)

What is required for a life to bear fruit?

Logos:

The LORD will guide you continually; And satisfy your soul in drought, And strengthen your bones; You shall be like a watered garden, And like a spring of water, whose waters do not fail. (Isaiah 58:11 NKJV)

Reflect and Respond

As I mature in my spiritual journey and learn and embrace more of God's will and ways, I am more aware of my daily need to make sure that my branch is well-watered and attached to the Vine. The Vine is what sustains branches and what they produce for others. What fertilizers do you think are essential for growing a healthy faith?

The entire Bible is FULL of many more wise, yoke-guiding principles. The book of Proverbs is especially rich with Scripture that shares practical, eternal wisdom for many aspects of life. Reading God's instructions and following them is the key to constructive growth, development, and change in our lives. But, following them all consistently, thoroughly, and well is a standard of perfection that is elusive to most. Thankfully, it is through our acknowledged mistakes and corrective actions that we can be refined.

FAITH-RELATED DRIVER #3

The Refining Process

Sleeping well can be a challenge in mid-life for a few reasons, and for me, one of them is putting my head on my pillow with thoughts of interactions from the day that didn't reflect Christ well. Such memories affect me and my sense of peace because they grieve the Holy Spirit within me. Over time, this sense of conviction has served as motivation for me to guard my tongue and consider my interactions, choices, and priorities. It's the sanctification process at work. Let's explore some encouraging verses that provide inspirational assurance when our non-fruit-bearing limbs are being cut or when we are being refined and are learning from our mistakes.

Logos:

Then I acknowledged my sin to you and did not cover up my iniquity. I said, "I will confess my transgressions to the LORD." And **you forgave the guilt** of my sin. (Psalm 32:5 NIV; emphasis mine)

Dear friends, if we don't feel guilty, we can come to God with **bold confidence**. (1 John 3:21 NLT; emphasis mine)

Do not be deceived: God cannot be mocked. A man reaps what he sows. Whoever sows to please their flesh, from the flesh will reap destruction; whoever sows to please the Spirit, from the Spirit will reap eternal life. (Galatians 6:7–8 NIV)

Reflect and Respond

What causes guilt?

Why might a sense of guilt interfere or impact our relationship with God?

In what ways is the acknowledgment of personal sin beneficial?

While it's possible to ignore sin, what are the dangers of doing so?

Logos:

Come close to God, and God will come close to you. Wash your hands, you sinners; purify your hearts, for your loyalty is divided between God and the world. (James 4:8 NLT; emphasis mine)

Confess your sins to each other and pray for each other **so that you may be healed**. The earnest prayer of a righteous person has great power and produces wonderful results. (James 5:16 NLT; emphasis mine)

Whoever conceals their sins does not prosper, but the **one who confesses and renounces them finds mercy.** (Proverbs 28:13 NIV; emphasis mine)

Repent, then, and turn to God, so that your sins may be wiped out, that times of **refreshing may come from the Lord**. (Acts 3:19 NIV; emphasis mine)

Reflect and Respond

Isn't it edifying to know that God welcomes us to draw close to Him and to be honest with Him about our issues and shortcomings?

Considering the verses above, what benefits are associated with the acknowledgement of sin?

Logos:

fixing our eyes on Jesus, the pioneer and **perfecter of faith**. For the joy set before him he endured the cross, scorning its shame, and sat down at the right hand of the throne of God. (Hebrews 12:2 NIV)

Reflect and Respond

How is Jesus the perfecter of our faith? How does that make you feel?

Logos:

For the **LORD disciplines those he loves**, and he punishes each one he accepts as his child. As you endure this divine discipline, remember that God is treating you as his own children. Who ever heard of a child who is never disciplined by its father? (Hebrews 12:6–7 NLT; emphasis mine)

But as **we have been approved by God to be entrusted with the gospel**, even so we speak, not as pleasing men, but God **who tests our hearts**. (1 Thessalonians 2:4 NKJV; emphasis mine)

We are therefore **Christ's ambassadors**, as though God were making his appeal through us. We implore you on Christ's behalf: Be reconciled to God. (2 Corinthians 5:20 NIV; emphasis mine)

You show that you are a letter from Christ, the result of our ministry, written not with ink but with the Spirit of the living God, not on tablets of stone but on tablets of human hearts. (2 Corinthians 3:3 NIV; emphasis mine)

Watch your life and doctrine closely. Persevere in them, because **if you do, you will save both yourself and your hearers.** (1 Timothy 4:16 NIV; emphasis mine)

Reflect and Respond

I don't think most people associate discipline or corrective action with positive feelings. Considering the verses above, how and why do you think the Lord disciplines those whom He loves? Why is that actually encouraging?

Who is instrumental in testing the heart of a believer? How do you think that is accomplished?

How would you define the word ambassador? What responsibilities come with such a role?

What is the result of living a Spirit-led life that demonstrates faithfulness, appreciation, and respect for God's Word, will, and ways?

Logos:

The faithful love of the LORD never ends! His mercies never cease. Great is his faithfulness; his mercies begin afresh each morning. (Lamentations 3:22—23 NLT)

For by a single offering He has perfected for all time those who are being sanctified. (Hebrews 10:14 ESV)

I love how the two verses above help to bring this section to fruition. God's faithfulness, love, and mercies never cease! When we "own" our shortcomings and share them with God, we can rest much more easily knowing that the dawn of a new day will bring a fresh start through Jesus Christ— The One Who is transforming and refining us. Praise be to God!

Conclusion

I'm not very consistent or dedicated to physical activity. At an annual medical appointment, my physician told me that I needed to consider exercise as a prescription and not a suggestion. She got my attention.

Likewise, I've also learned that seeking God's will and ways by reading His Word, praying, and internalizing it through an application and review process is the holistic prescription I need to use consistently in order to create the type of legacy I want to leave.

My priority is to sow seeds for God's kingdom and contribute to the yield of a perpetual crop that has the capacity to impact, benefit, and provide generations of people everywhere with eternal dividends. The following verses offer insight, motivation, and encouragement for the pursuit of that goal.

Logos:

Don't store up treasures here on earth, where moths eat them and rust destroys them, and where thieves break in and steal. Store your treasures in heaven, where moths and rust cannot destroy, and thieves do not break in and steal. Wherever your treasure is, there the desires of your heart will also be. (Matthew 6:19—21 NLT)

Reflect and Respond

How would you describe the difference between treasures on earth and treasures in heaven?

Describe how the desires of one's heart contribute to motivations and choices in life?

Logos:

The world and its desires pass away, but whoever does the will of God lives forever. (1 John 2:17 NIV)

In this way they will lay up treasure for themselves as a firm foundation for the coming age, so that they may take hold of the life that is truly life. (1 Timothy 6:19 NIV)

Reflect and Respond

What is your understanding about the longevity of life in the world?

What is the coming age?

How would you describe the life that is truly life?

Logos:

His master replied, "Well done, good and faithful servant! You have been faithful with a few things; I will put you in charge of many things. Come and share your master's happiness!" (Matthew 25:23 NIV)

Reflect and Respond

The verse above is a portion of the parable of the talents that is shared in Matthew 25:14—30. Please read it for complete context.

What blessings come from investing and sharing what we know about God and His will and ways with others?

What thoughts come to mind when you consider all of the implications of the parable?

Logos:

So then, my dear friends, stand firm and steady. Keep busy always in your work for the Lord, since you know that nothing you do in the Lord's service is ever useless. (1 Corinthians 15:58 GNT)

Reflect and Respond

Although not everyone has a professional role in ministry, how can believers keep busy in their work for the Lord in their daily lives?

How does it make you feel that whatever we do to bring glory to God has a purpose?

Logos:

Therefore, since we are surrounded by such a great cloud of witnesses, let us throw off everything that hinders and the sin that so easily entangles. And **let us run with perseverance the race marked out for us, fixing our eyes on Jesus, the pioneer and perfecter of faith**. (Hebrews 12:1–2a NIV; emphasis mine)

I have fought the good fight, I have finished the race, and I have remained faithful. (2 Timothy 4:7 NLT)

Reflect and Respond

How is Jesus the pioneer and perfecter of our faith? How does it make you feel that we have help, support, and guidance in our faith journeys?

Races can be long or short, and the pace can vary. What does it mean to remain faithful, and how does that contribute to how we finish?

Logos:

And we also thank God continually because, when you received the word of God, which you heard from us, you accepted it not as a human word, but as it actually is, the **word of God, which is indeed at work in you who believe**. (1 Thessalonians 2:13 NIV; emphasis mine)

Being confident of this, that he who began a good work in you will carry it on to completion until the day of Christ Jesus. (Philippians 1:6 NIV)

Reflect and Respond

I'm grateful that God is at work (present tense!) in me, and that He will continue to be actively involved in the work that He is doing in my life. I'm certainly cognizant of my myriad shortcomings, and I'm glad to be enrolled in His Master class and management plan. I highly recommend it. Participation in His training program is a legacy-builder that has universal benefits. Its continuing education and professional development opportunities are relevant and free, and it contributes to the type of legacy that I want to leave—one that honors and respects God first and foremost as well as benefits others and myself.

What kind of legacy would you like to leave? What priorities and pursuits would contribute to it?

Afterword

Not to us, LORD, not to us, but to your name be the glory,
because of your love and faithfulness. (Psalm 115:1 NIV)

About the Author

The author of two other interactive, faith-based books, *The SQ Factor* and *The ID Factor*, Amy's passion is to share the empowering truth, grace, and hope found in God's Word in simple, accessible, and culturally-relevant ways.

04090118-00836562

Printed in the United States
by Baker & Taylor Publisher Services